TRANSFORMATION
THE YOUNG GIRLS GUIDE TO WOMANHOOD

LANE BIRD

illustrated by Micah Amaro

TRANSFORMATION

THE YOUNG GIRLS GUIDE TO WOMANHOOD

LANE BIRD

Gemlight Publishing LLC

Gulfport, Mississippi

Notice of Copyright

All rights reserved. No part of this publication may be reproduced in any form, or by any means, electronic or mechanical, including photocopying, recording, or any information browsing, storage, or retrieval system, without permission in writing from the publisher.

Edited By: Sarah Nguyen

Illustrated Cover by : Micah Amaro
Printed in the United States of America
Available from https://www.gemlightpublishing.com and other retail outlets
ISBN 978-1-736-7934-2-8

Copyright © 2021
LANE BIRD
TRANSFORMATION

Dedication

To my son, Terance, who is always supportive.
To my late mother, Doris V. Hyde-Bird, and my late grandmother, Viola R. Hyde, who watched over me each and every day. I grew from the life lessons you taught me.
Last but not least, to all the girls who have transformed into beautiful butterflies.

Acknowledgments

I would like to thank the person who gave me the idea to write this book, Erica Sherrill. Erica has been an inspiration to me in so many ways.

I would like to thank my son for listening to me and being my critic.

Thank you, Vicki Silas, for your encouraging words and prayers.

Thank you, Jennifer Hairston, for being my second mom and being a positive influence.

Thank you to all my family and friends who gave me the encouragement and prayers to complete this book.

Thank you to all the beautiful, lovely, intelligent, awesome young butterflies who will find who they are in this wonderful transformation to adulthood.

I Love You

Table of Contents

Author's Note 09

Introduction 10

WHO AM I? 12

WHAT'S HAPPENING TO MY BODY? 14

SHOULD I DATE? 27

EVERYONE IS DOING DRUGS, SHOULD I? 45

ABSTINENCE CONTRACT 59

REFERENCE 61

MY JOURNAL 62

Author's Note

Hello, beautiful Queens!!

Life has caught you by surprise, but don't be afraid, I am here to have a girl chat with you. I wrote this book especially for you, and we will be discussing all the goodies. You will learn to understand the physical and emotional changes that are taking place in your body when puberty starts. Remember, this is a natural and wonderful process into young adulthood then womanhood. Transforming can be confusing and scary, but every girl in this world has gone through this process. It is also important to know that it can be different for each person. You will see changes in your body, thoughts, and feelings about the opposite sex.

We will take a look at each stage, from the beginning when the body starts to change on the inside, to when physical changes start to appear on the outside. I will provide you with tips on how to take care of yourself during your monthly cycle. We will discuss some symptoms that can make you feel out of whack with reality. Remember, it's okay to feel this way! It is all a part of nature taking its course.

We will also talk about dating and boys and how to know if you are ready for a relationship. Handling all these transformations properly and talking to your mother or another woman you trust will get you through this wonderful time smoothly. I cannot promise you that you will not feel uncomfortable and sometimes frustrated, but you will survive, and it will get easier. I want you to see yourself as a beautiful butterfly;

now, let's begin...

Introduction

A small caterpillar was born. With some difficulty, she finally learned how to crawl. Everyday, she would crawl on the ground, from one place to another. One day, she was tired of crawling, so she decided to climb a tree. The caterpillar chose to climb a tree with a large trunk and dewy leaves. It was the same tree she had played under for years.

The caterpillar climbed and climbed, but she continued to slip and fall; she could not move forward. But she did not give up, and step by step, little by little, she managed to climb up the tree successfully. She climbed her way to branches so high, she could see the whole valley. The view was wonderful. From the branch, the caterpillar was able to breathe in peace.

Then, the caterpillar then turned into a cocoon.

After a long period of time, the caterpillar bursted through the cocoon. She was now a beautiful blue butterfly, but she thought she was still a caterpillar. Something was weighing her down; she couldn't move as she did before. She felt heavy and uncomfortable. A gust of wind pushed her backward, and she decided to return to the branch where the transformation happened. But this time, the climb was harder; moving forward seemed impossible. Since she thought she was still a caterpillar, the butterfly stood and looked up at the branch. Then, she started to cry.

A beautiful and wise yellow butterfly heard her cry and approached her. The yellow butterfly perched on a flower, and for a while, she looked at the blue butterfly without saying anything. When the blue butterfly's crying subsided, the yellow butterfly said, "What happened?" "I can't climb up that branch. Before, even though it was hard, I could do it."

"If you can't climb up the branch, maybe you can try flying to it."

The yellow butterfly started to fly and the blue butterfly watched, amazed at the yellow butterfly's movement. She then reflected on the yellow butterfly's movement. She began to understand that she was no longer a caterpillar; she was now a butterfly with wings. She realized that perhaps her heavy wings could be useful. The blue butterfly opened her wings and closed her eyes. She then felt the wind caressing them. She now knows that these wings were now a part of her. Finally, she accepted that she was no longer a caterpillar; therefore, she could not continue to live as such, crawling on the ground.

Going through puberty can be fearful and painful, but with help and understanding, you will begin to accept yourself just like the butterfly did. You will continue to live and embrace yourself as a young adult, and not the child you used to be. This might take some time, and it could be difficult at times. If you have someone in your life that can mentor you the same way the yellow butterfly mentored the blue butterfly, then go to this person for help. If not, then you can view this book and my words as that "mentor" for you. Trust your mom, aunt, grandmother, or a female figure you admire to help you get through this transformation. They will be able to help because they went through it too.

Now, let's begin navigating your
journey from being a girl to a young woman.

WHO AM I?

Everything you do is built on how you perceive it. Having a positive mindset and knowing who you are will help make your transformation into womanhood a beautiful experience. Start by saying this every morning: "I am beautiful, confident, and valuable." Try saying this in the bathroom while you are getting ready for your day. Look in the mirror and say these positive affirmations to yourself. Soon, your subconscious mind will repeat these positive affirmations without you having to say it aloud.

HERE ARE SOME MORE POSITIVE, LOVING WORDS (AFFIRMATIONS):

I am happy.

Today is a wonderful, positive day.

I am beautiful.

I love me.

I am blessed, and I am a blessing to all I meet.

THINK OF SOME KIND, LOVING WORDS TO SAY TO YOURSELF EACH DAY.

-
-
-
-

Now that you've listed some affirmations, pick one that you can use daily that will help you think positively and will help you achieve success in anything you desire. You can use affirmations to help you get through a tough class or a serious talk with your parents or even a difficult decision about a friend. Remember, affirmations are actions we desire to manifest.

Now that you have figured out some of your favorite affirmations, the next section will help you learn more about you. Knowing what you like, and dislike is good, but understanding why is important. Getting to know yourself is super important during this journey to womanhood.

I know it can be complicated learning about all that you like and dislike. Taking a personality quiz is a quick, easy, and fun way to do that. Let's get started!

1. My favorite food is…
   - ☐ Pizza
   - ☐ Chicken
   - ☐ Pasta
   - ☐ Other _____

2. I usually like watching _____ movies.
   - ☐ Scary
   - ☐ Romance
   - ☐ Action
   - ☐ Drama

3. I like _____ during my spare time.
   - ☐ Making TikTok videos
   - ☐ Playing video games (Ex: Fortnite, Among Us, Roblox)
   - ☐ Reading
   - ☐ Singing

4. I am working on …
   - ☐ Accepting myself
   - ☐ Expressing myself
   - ☐ Improving myself
   - ☐ Serving others

5. I like wearing _____

- [ ] Joggers
- [ ] Jeans
- [ ] Tights
- [ ] Casual dresses

6. How do you tend to act in social situations?

- [ ] Tell stories
- [ ] Crack jokes
- [ ] Don't know what to say
- [ ] Get in a debate

Great job! Wasn't that FUN? You learned a little bit more about yourself, and that only took a few seconds! You will learn more about yourself as you grow older, but this quiz was just a quick and fun way to get you started.

What's Happening To My Body?
Stage One - Egg

At birth, a girl's pair of ovaries contain up to 1,000,000 follicles, (hollow balls of cells), each with an immature egg in the center. These eggs stay inactive until puberty begins.

I am Glad You Asked!
Let's start by defining puberty.
Puberty is the process of physical changes by which adolescents reach sexual maturity. This means you will be capable of reproduction. This also pertains to bodily changes (Webster). Your ovaries will get bigger, and your body will start to produce two hormones, estrogen, and progesterone. Estrogen causes your breast to grow and helps your vagina, uterus, and fallopian tubes develop.

With girls, puberty usually starts around 11 years of age, but it can also start as early as 6 or 7 years of age. As you start noticing changes in your body, you will realize that while some are exciting, others can be frightening. Here are some examples of the changes you might face: You might first notice thin, fine hair under your armpits or pubic area. Your breast may start to develop and feel tender. You may notice your hips becoming more rounded, and you might get a more defined waist. A vaginal discharge can also occur because of an increase in the mucous produced in the vagina.

While all these are normal, they can sometimes make you feel insecure or embarrassed. Don't be! Know that every girl is going through it or will go through it. Talk with a trusted female figure in your life if something is happening with your body that frightens you or talk to someone your age such as a friend or family member. Ask her if she is going through something similar.

What Is That Smell?

Reaching puberty means you might start to smell a little musty, so you will have to start using deodorant, as well as feminine hygiene products. Hair will start to grow under your armpit, in your pubic area, and also on your leg. Bacteria, sweat, and other undesirable substances will cling onto these hair; thus, making you produce odors that are very unpleasant. Sweating and body odor are common when you exercise, or if you are too warm. They're also common when you're feeling nervous, anxious, or stressed. Sweat glands have always been a part of your body, but puberty causes these glands to secrete different chemicals into the sweat, causing a stronger smelling odor. It is important for these areas to stay cleaned and washed so they don't produce odor.

Taking Care Of Your Body and Skin

Staying Fresh & Clean:

These are a lot of feminine hygiene products out there that are made specifically for girls to help them keep their odors under control. Try out a few and see which ones work best with your body. If you need some suggestions, here are examples of some deodorants and feminine washes that can help you feel clean:

Dove has a line of deodorants for girls active in sports: Advance Care Go Fresh Rejuvenate Antiperspirant Deodorant, Advance Care Go Fresh Apple & White Tea, and Dove Advanced Care Sensitive Anti-Perspirant Deodorant.

Arm & Hammer: Essentials Solid Deodorant, Essentials Solid Deodorant Fresh, and Essential Solid Deodorant Unscented.

Deodorant Stones of America: Thai Crystal.

Feminine Hygiene:
Summer's Eve: Cleansing Wash, Cleansing Cloths (Sensitive). Disposable Flushable Wipes.

Nair: Hair Removal Products.

Avon: Skin so Soft, and Fresh & Smooth Body Hair Removal Cream.

Acne: Pimples Everywhere

Now that you have an idea of where to start when it comes to hygiene products, let's talk about another annoying factor of adolescence: acne. Acne is another part of puberty. Teens and preteens are likely to get acne because of the hormonal changes that come with puberty. When bacteria, skin oil, and hormones interact, it causes pimples to form on the face and upper body. Acne can be treated by washing infected locations twice a day. You must keep your face clean, but do NOT wash your face with a bar of body soap. Always use a facial cleanser that is meant for the face and moisturize right after. Do not use the same towel to wipe your face as you do on the rest of your body, this is a good way to spread bacteria. Instead, keep a separate towel just for your face and make sure to wash it often.

Products to Help with Acne:
Botanical Effects by MaryKay: Cleansing Gel, Refreshing Toner, Moisturizing Gel.

MaryKay Clear Proof Acne System: Clarifying Cleansing Gel, Blemish Control Toner, Acne Treatment Gel, Oil-Free Moisturizer for Acne-Prone Skin.

Retinoids: Prescribed as creams, gels, and lotion to prevent clogging of hair follicles.

Whether it's the first time you notice a weird smell coming from your body or the first time you see a stubborn red bump pop up on your forehead, it is important to keep track of these changes. Get a journal or planner, and write down any changes you notice with your body. Remember, this is normal. You can also write in this book if you prefer.

The first time you notice:

DATE	HAIR	ODORS	PIMPLES	BREAST	HOW DID YOU FEEL?

What are some new products you have tried? Which ones do you like? Which ones did you dislike?

> What's This In My Way?

> Breast:
> You start to see signs of breast development, and it is kind of freaking you out. Once again, totally normal. It starts with a small mass under your nipples. Like a mound or a nub, then they will gradually grow bigger as you get older. They can be very tender and sore at first. They will also itch as your skin stretches. The areola (the area around the nipple) may get darker and larger, and the nipple may become erect or stick out. During your monthly period, the changes in your breasts may include swelling, pain, tenderness, and in some cases, changes in breast texture, with the breasts feeling lumpy.
>
> It's time for you and mom to go bra shopping...
> Despite their names, training bras don't train the breasts. They are called that because they will help you become familiar with wearing a bra. They are usually worn when breast buds first appear. They do not offer padding or support, and they should be replaced when your breasts begin to fully develop. If you don't know what kind of bra you should buy, talk to your mom or a trusted female figure. If this makes you uncomfortable, ask a friend or check online for helpful articles. Here are some examples of bras you might see:

Here are some examples of bras you might see:

Training bras are ideal when breasts first start to develop. They are comfortable and usually come in fun colors or patterns.

Sports Bras are a must for girls who are active or play sports. A good sports bra will offer extra protection against chafing of the nipple. Sports bras restrict the movement of the breast by compressing them against the skin.

Soft Cup Bras are a good choice for girls with small to medium-sized breasts.

Underwire Bras come with a flexible wire that helps lift the breast. They offer jiggle support for girls with large breasts.

Bras come in many colors, sizes, and comfort. You do not need to spend a lot of money on a good bra. You can go to stores like Target or Walmart and find a good quality and inexpensive bra. While most girls find the thought of bras intimidating, others will find it exciting. If you are in the latter group, remember that training bras are usually not "sexy." So, don't be too mad at your mom if she buys you some plain ones to get you started. Although your main objective is support and comfort, you will find that some training bras can be stylish and colorful as well.

BRAS CHECKLIST

WHAT DO YOU WANT IN A BRA?
_____
_____

What Color?
_____
_____

What Style?
_____
_____

Do you want something SPORTY or LACY?
_____
_____

Do you need support? For your back or front?
_____
_____

Have you discussed your choices with your mom or a responsible adult?
_____
_____

Stage Two – Larva (caterpillar)

Having fun, experiencing, getting to know your surroundings.

> I'm Bleeding, OH My! WHY?

> Your body is getting ready for the next stage...
> Your Period (Menstruation):
> Your period consists of blood and tissue that build up as the lining of your uterus sheds each month. When you were born, there were hundreds of thousands of eggs (ova) inside the ovaries. Each month, when you reach puberty, these hormones will cause an egg to start maturing and be released from the ovary. This is called ovulation. The egg moves along the fallopian tube toward the uterus. The lining of the uterus becomes thick and soft with blood and tissue. This happens just in case the egg is fertilized. It would implant itself into the lining of the uterus and grow. The egg can only be fertilized when it is joined with sperm from a male.
> When the egg is not fertilized, it is reabsorbed back into the body. The uterus's lining is not needed, so it goes away and is released by your body through your vagina. This process is your menstruation or period. It can flow light, heavy, or in between. Menstrual blood can also vary in color. It can be different shades of red, from light to dark. You may sometimes see dark clumps or clots of blood; this is normal. Your period may be heavy the first day, then it will get lighter as the days go on.
>
> Periods usually last between three and five days. It is normal to have periods that are shorter or longer than that timeframe; it can go up to seven days. It is also normal if your period does not start on the exact day each month.
>
> Menstrual cramps can also occur, and the pain-level varies. Some girls will get cramps that hurt so badly, they can't get out of bed, while other girls do not get any cramps at all. If your stomach starts hurting at the start of your period, ask your mom or a trusted adult for some pain reliever such as Aleve or Ibuprofen. If the pain gets to be unbearable, talk to your doctor.

TRANSFORMATION THE YOUNG GIRL GUIDE TO WOMANHOOD

Taking Care of your Period:
There are many different products you can use during your time of the month, from sanitary pads to tampons to menstrual cups. Some girls prefer one product over the other, while others like to use different products depending on how they are feeling. For example, a girl may prefer pads over tampons but if she knows she is going to go swimming the next day, then she will use a tampon. Try different products and find the one that is right for you.

What To Use?

Tampons:
A tampon goes inside the vagina to soak up the blood before it leaves your body. This can take practice and may feel uncomfortable at first. Always use a pantyliner with tampons because tampons can sometimes leak. Tampons can have a plastic or cardboard covering that makes it easier for you to put the tampon in. This is the applicator. Do not leave the applicator inside your vagina. All tampons have a string at the end. You pull on this string to help take the tampon out when it needs to be changed. Change your tampon at least every four to eight hours. I recommend not using a tampon when it's time to go to bed because you should not leave it in for the entire night.

Tampons are ideal when you know you will be in the water. For example, if you know you will be swimming or if you play a watersport. On your heavier days, use a "super" tampon, and as the flow gets lighter, use a "regular" tampon.

Pads:
Pads stick on the inside of your underwear and soak up the blood that comes out through the vagina. A sticky strip holds them in place on your underwear. Some pads are thinner for days when your period is light, and some are thicker when you are bleeding more. You can also use these thicker pads at night when you sleep. Check your pad every couple of hours during the day to see if it needs changing. You should change it before it gets soaked or starts to smell. No one can tell if you are wearing a pad, so don't worry about that. If you are concerned about the smell, then change your pad often. Do not use scented or deodorant pads since they can irritate your skin.

Menstrual cups:
Menstrual cups are small cups that you insert into your vagina to collect blood. Some cups are one-time use only. Others can be emptied, washed, and reused.

If you are not sure which products you should start with, do not be afraid to ask your mother and/or a physician for some guidance.

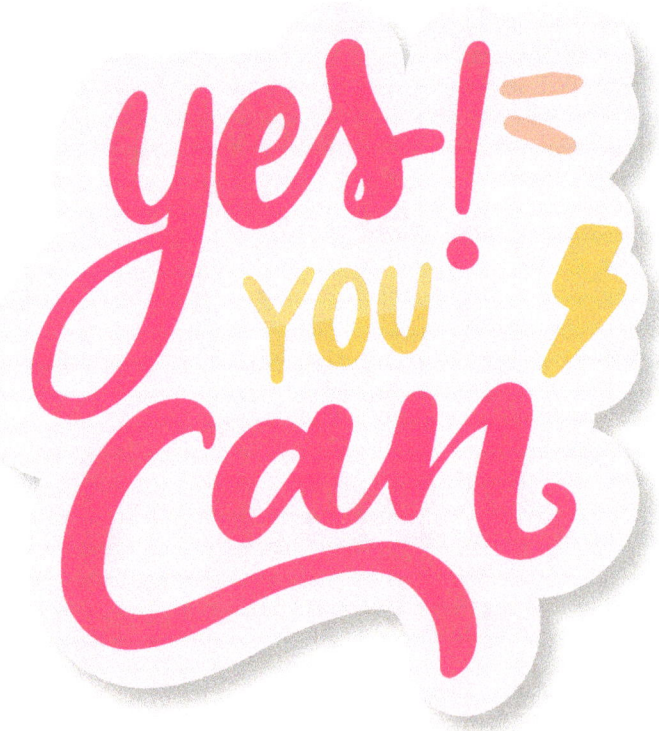

Stage Three – Pupa (cocoon)

Learning, growing, adapting, and becoming the woman you are meant to be.

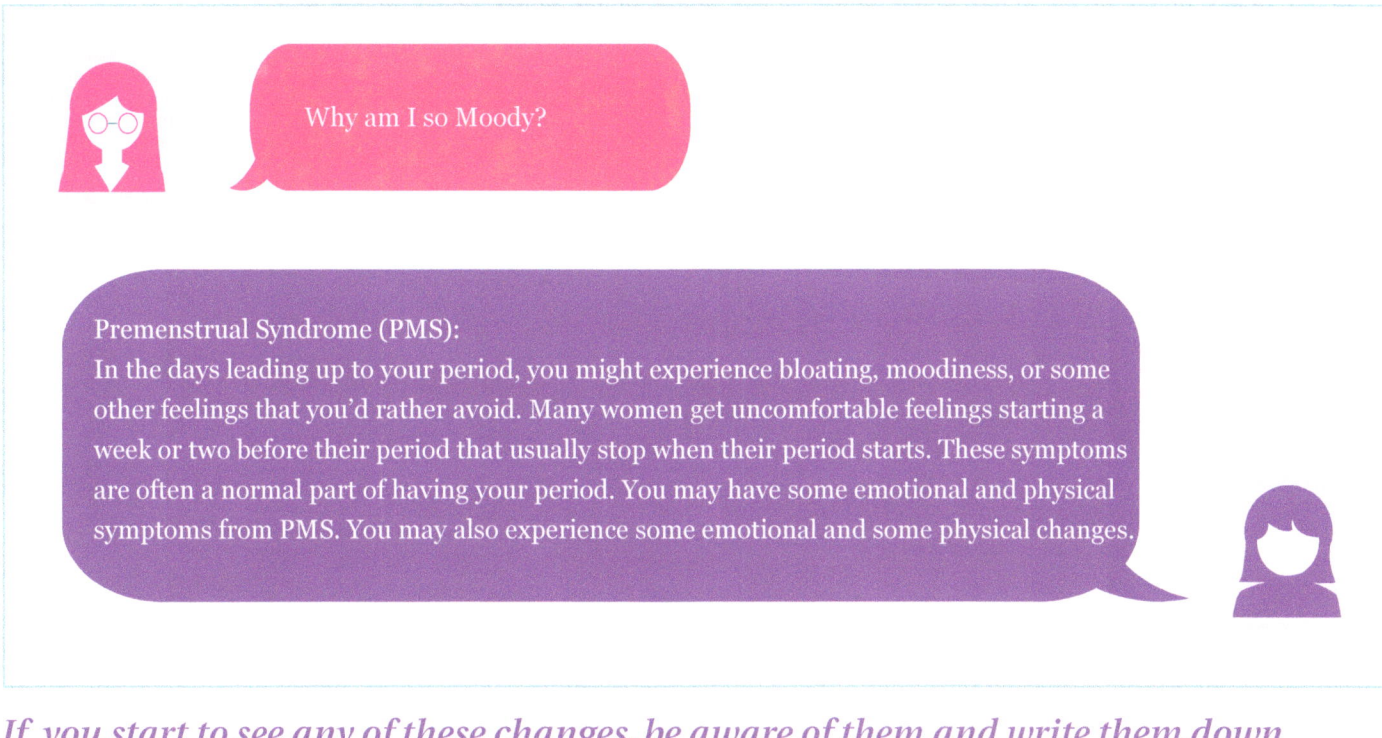

Why am I so Moody?

Premenstrual Syndrome (PMS):
In the days leading up to your period, you might experience bloating, moodiness, or some other feelings that you'd rather avoid. Many women get uncomfortable feelings starting a week or two before their period that usually stop when their period starts. These symptoms are often a normal part of having your period. You may have some emotional and physical symptoms from PMS. You may also experience some emotional and some physical changes.

If you start to see any of these changes, be aware of them and write them down below.

Emotional changes:
_____
_____

Physical changes:
_____
_____

HELP ME!

Tips to help with PMS:

Eat a healthy diet: Consume foods that are high in calcium, fruits, vegetables, and complex carbohydrates (found in whole-grain bread, pasta, and cereals). Stay away from salt the few days before your period to help with bloating. Drink less caffeine (found in soda, tea, and coffee) to feel less crabby and ease breast soreness. Eat small, frequent meals rather than a few big ones. Make sure you are getting enough physical activity every day (not just during your period).

Yoga and meditation: These activities can help with soreness in the body and irritation in the mind.

Sleep: Make sure you get enough sleep. Try to go to bed and get up at the same time every day.

Keep a calendar and mark when your period starts and when the last day was. Menstrual cycles usually last about 28 days. This means there are 28 days (give or take) between your last period and your next period. Once you get your period, you are physically able to become pregnant. Which means you and your mom, or a responsible adult will need to make an appointment to see a gynecologist. On your first visit, you will not need a pelvic exam. The gynecologists will do a regular health exam and will talk to you about your body and answer any questions that you may have.

1st MONTH	2nd MONTH	3rd MONTH	4th MONTH
BEFORE CYCLE			
AFTER CYCLE			

Reflection

1. Do you recall where you were when you noticed spotting?

   _____
   _____
   _____

2. How did you feel? Scared? Excited? Confused?

   _____
   _____
   _____

3. Who did you tell first?

   _____
   _____
   _____

Going into Adulthood

Adolescence: Am I ready?

This is the period following the onset of puberty during which a young person develops from a child into an adult. These are the years between 13 and 19 years of age. There are three stages to adolescence. I will explain the first two here and then we will dive into the last stage a bit later in the book.

- Early Adolescence

This stage occurs between ages 10 to 14. This is when puberty usually begins. This is when you become aware of your rapidly changing body and start to worry about your physical appearance. Relationships with close friends become more important than family relationships. This can also be the time where many teens start to act out.

- Middle Adolescence

This is the second stage that occurs from age 15 to 17. Puberty has passed by this time. You are extremely concerned with how you look, and you think others are concerned, too. You might spend large amounts of time grooming, exercising, and modifying your physical appearance. You may worry about sexual attractiveness.

You might complain about how your parents are preventing you from becoming independent, and you might even withdraw from them. This is when you try to assert your independence by not cleaning your room or picking up an annoying habit.

Peer pressure can come from all directions, the media, parents, other family members, and friends. This is the time when you must trust your parents and listen to what they are saying. They only have your best interest in mind. They want you to get through this stage in your life so you can become a productive, well-rounded citizen.

SHOULD I DATE?

The Attraction

You might find yourself being interested in boys now. Now that you have a better understanding of your body and how to handle those pesky period days, we are going to talk about boys. Remember, boys mature later than girls. While you might be interested in romantic movies, songs, and books, the guy you are crushing on might only have video games on his mind. This does not mean that all boys are immature, and all girls are mature, it is just that girls tend to (on average) mature faster than boys.

As you start to feel emotionally connected to someone, you might want to explore physical closeness as well. Intimacy is a form of closeness, and it can include sexual intercourse. While your hormones may urge you to do otherwise, make sure to take things slow. Remember to protect your temple. The temple is YOU, your body. Your body is a temple of the Holy Spirit who is in you; therefore, you must honor God with your body. Keep your body clean and presentable. Also, be mindful of whom you invite into your temple. If they are not responsible, loyal, trustworthy, and God-fearing, they can't enter. When someone is worthy of your time, and they respect you, they will wait. You do not need a boy to tell you that you are beautiful or sexy. You already know this. Enjoy your new self, learn who you are, learn about your body. Have fun, laugh, and play.

Love is patient; love is kind. It does not envy; it does not boast; it is not proud. It is not rude; it is not self-seeking, it is not easily angered, it keeps no record of wrongs. It always protects, always trusts, always hope perseveres. Love never fails (1 Corinthians 13:4-8).

The meaning of dating

Depending on your age, dating could mean different things to different age groups. For example, for a 6th grader, dating could mean sitting next to that special someone at lunch or hanging out at recess. 8th graders might view dating as texting, talking on the phone, or sharing social media images with one person. If you are thinking about going on a date with a boy you like but you do not know what to do, try going to the movies or meeting at the mall in groups. Sometimes, bringing other friends along can be a safe and healthy way to interact with members of the opposite sex. If you want, you can also ask another couple to join you for a double date. If you have gone on several group dates and are considering one-on-one dates, ask yourself: Am I emotionally mature and responsible enough to go on one?

Signs to know I'm NOT ready to date

- **Struggle to talk about feelings**

Mature girls can explain and process complicated feelings.

- **Give up your space**

Mature girls know they need time alone. Whether that "me-time" means going to the gym, or curling up with a good book. Doing things on your own will encourage and preserve your sense of independence.

- **Don't like to compromise**

Mature girls do not think that it is their way or no way. They know how to sit down and listen to suggestions on what can make a situation better for both parties.

- **Get defensive**

Mature girls do not get defensive at the first sign of criticism. Mature girls are able to listen and take in what their partner is saying, even if it is hard for them to hear. No one should feel as if they need to walk on eggshells in fear of upsetting their partner.

- **Need constant contact with a partner**

Mature girls do not need constant contact in their relationship; they have their own lives.

- **Give up your happiness**

Mature girls understand the importance of their happiness, and if they are not happy in a relationship, then they should not be in one.

- **Give up self-respect**

Mature girls don't allow their relationship to take away their self-respect. They don't allow their partner to speak to them negatively.

- **Can't make decisions**

Mature girls are able to make decisions in relationships, and their partners should always be respectful and be considerate of those decisions. And vice versa!

Emotional Responsibility

Relationships thrive when both partners are kind, accepting, compassionate, and empathetic. Yet, you have to learn to be kind, accepting, and compassionate toward yourself first; you cannot abandon yourself. If you can't be kind to yourself, how are you going to be kind to others? When you truly love yourself, you will understand that you are responsible for your happiness. When you can make yourself happy, you are not depending on your partner to make you happy which will make the relationship feel less burdensome.

Do I really like him?

You might think you like that boy in your homeroom class, but how do you really know? To help you get a better idea, take this quick quiz:

Do you have your eyes on a special little boy?

 Yes

No

 Maybe

1. What makes him so special?

_____

_____

2. Do you think (truthfully) you are mature enough to date? Why or why not?

_____

_____

3. What makes YOU happy?

_____
_____
_____

4. What does respect mean to you?

_____
_____
_____

5. What are you looking for in another person?

_____
_____
_____

6. How is your communication with him?

_____
_____
_____
_____

7. What do you both talk about?

_____
_____
_____
_____

This is who I am: Loving Me, Being Me

Boys, Boys, Boys.

You want to go to school; he wants to hang out with friends; you want to build a financial future; he wants to spend every dime on $100+ tennis shoes and the latest fashion trends. His idea of a date is taking you to McDonald's and making out in the back seat of his car. Run, Run, Run.

You are better and should want more for your future. The choices we make can either bring us up or bring us down. Make the smart choice. Here are some things to keep in mind:

1. Make sure you are ready. There is no rule that states you must date at a certain age. If you are uncomfortable with the idea of dating, then don't.
2. Set boundaries. Always set mental boundaries for yourself. Otherwise, you may find yourself getting into situations you don't want to be in.
3. Try group dating. You might feel a little intimidated by the idea of one-on-one dating. If that is true, then try going on a date with another couple you trust.
4. Keep your relationship OFF social media.
5. Watch out for red flags. Don't brush off warning signs that could lead to a potentially bad relationship. Like your partner insulting or belittling you or others, forcing you to do things you don't want to do, or invading your privacy.
6. Always be yourself. Being yourself is an important aspect of dating. Get to know each other better before getting into a serious relationship.
7. Tell someone (parent or trusted mature friend) about your plans. Always think about your safety. Let the third party know what time the date starts and where you are going. Also let them know when you expect to be back. If the date goes longer than expected, let them know you are okay.

"Love is the condition in which the happiness of another person is essential to your own."

> I'm Dating now. What's NEXT?

If you decide to date and feel you are emotionally and mentally mature enough to date, the next question might be where you should go on your date. If you are asked this question by your date, what are you going to say? Depending on the situation, does your friend have a job? You should probably choose to go somewhere he can afford. This is especially important if you are younger, and your date does not make a lot of money or does not have a job yet. Always be confident and know what you want. When you are asked where you want to go, know where you want to go and what you want to do. Be familiar with the restaurants in your area.

If your date asks you, "Where would you like to go on our date?" then you should have an answer. For example, say "I would like to go to Olive Garden, Apple Bee's, Outback, Chili's, or the Hibachi Grill." If your date can't take you to a nice restaurant or somewhere decent, it doesn't necessarily mean he doesn't like you; it could mean he can't afford to take you to that place. Try to come with more affordable ideas like going to get coffee at a coffee shop or grabbing ice cream somewhere so you can both sit and talk with people around.

Places to go on your one-on-one or group date:

- Bowling
- Miniature golf
- Water Park
- Amusement Park
- Zoo
- Concerts

- Dave and Buster
- Beach
- Fishing Pond
- Animal shelter
- Museum
- Arcade
- Carnival

Activities to do on your one-on-one or group date:

- Do a puzzle
- Read books together (2-person book club)
- Play in the snow
- Stargazing
- Roller Skating
- Top Swing
- Ice Skating

Dating is about getting to know each other's likes and dislikes. How is the vibe between you and your date? When you are with him, do you feel comfortable and relaxed in his presence? Does he make you laugh? Is he confident in himself? Can he listen and talk? Can he communicate well? Finding out these things on your date can be fun. Just be yourself and have fun, but stay observant.

> "Spend time alone in objective thought as you consider the direction of your life."
>
> *-I Ching*

Relationship

 "Am I really in a relationship?"

We think the main reason for being in a relationship is because of love, but you will need more than love for a relationship to work.

1. Trust – Is the most important factor in a relationship. For your relationship to be healthy and stable, you must trust each other. Trust people until they give you a reason not to trust them; don't look for reasons to not trust. Just believe if they are doing something untrustworthy, those actions will be revealed.

2. Honesty – This is the second most important thing. A relationship is not built on lies and false hope. Being honest leads to good communication. When you tell the truth, the story is always the same. This means you don't have to remember what to say if you are telling the truth. Even if you ask someone about something they did five years ago, the story should never change.

3. Respect – You should never give up who you are for anyone. If you cannot be yourself around someone, then they do not deserve you. Don't waste your time; move on.

4. Communication – You must express your needs, feelings, and expectations clearly and calmly. You must solve all issues whether they are big or small with love and respect. If you can talk to the person you are with and this person respects your voice and hears you, then this will build a strong relationship.

5. Loyalty – Staying faithful to your partner and the relationship is a crucial building block for other values. You have to want to be in a relationship and commit to it for it to work. Don't stay in a relationship if your partner is not loyal; he might say, "I love you. I won't do that again," but he will.

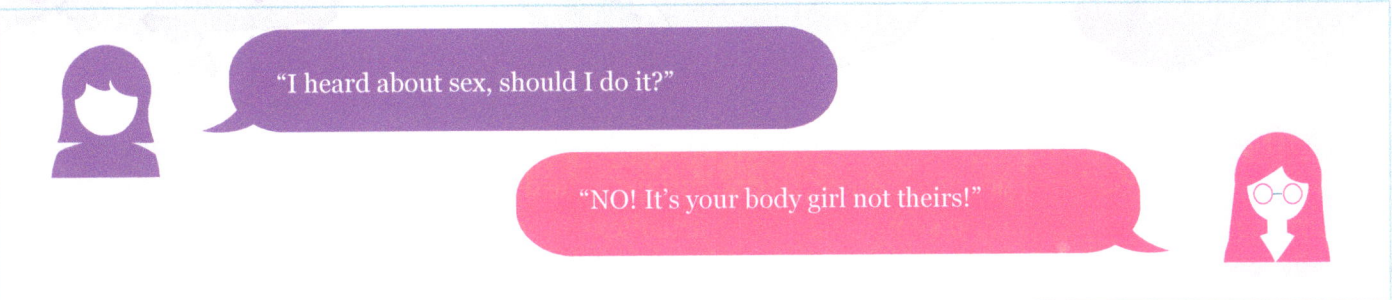

Temptation

This goes back to your temple; you are a queen, respecting yourself and wanting someone who is respectful, kind, loving, and willing to wait for you is crucial. God commands and demands there shouldn't be a hint of sexual immorality among us, which is so easy for us to do, right? WRONG. If you have never experienced sex, you aren't missing anything; it is a desire and curiosity. When you are with that special friend that you care for so much, it can be tempting when he kisses you and hugs you or even holds your hand. But you must respect yourself enough to wait.

Do you ever think, "If I don't do it, will he leave?" If he leaves, then let him walk away because he is not the one. Or he will go with someone who is willing to do it. Just be observant and open your ears. Listen to your friends who may be engaging in some form of sexual activity and hear what they don't want you to know. Most of them are in demanding relationships. They are jealous, and they act differently. Guys will run after someone they can't have quicker than they will someone they know will have sex with them. Once you start having sex, you will be called names; boys love to brag about who they have been with and that's not good. Because boys are not mature, they will sleep with anyone. Girls tend to be more emotional, which means they care about who they sleep with. This is not to say that all boys and all girls are the same; it is merely an observation. This is why you must get to know someone as a friend first; this will give your insight into how they think about certain situations.

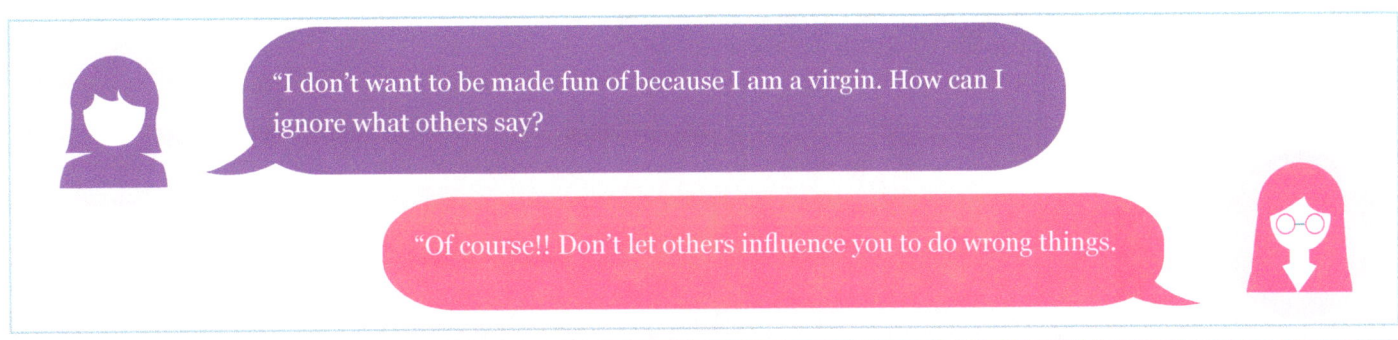

Let's talk about the Book of Instructions, "The Bible." The book that tells us what we should and shouldn't do so we can live a blessed and prosperous life, full of joy, peace, and happiness. Even though it gives us instructions, it also gives us choices. The only thing we must know is when to make the right choice. The Lord has some serious rules about sexual immorality, and we are going to talk about some of them. I do not want you to think that our Lord and Savior does not believe in relationships or he doesn't want you to have fun. He wants you to enjoy your teen years, but He also knows that certain activities can change the course and path that is already planned for you. He believes in love and relationships. In fact, there is a whole book in the bible called "Song of Songs." The first relationship in the bible was Adam & Eve; then, there were others, Naomi & Boaz, Shari & Abraham, and Mary & Joseph. Some were not good because they were sexually involved or disobedient. Like Samson & Delilah, and Ado & Lot. You can read about how Solomon disobeyed God and married whom he was not supposed to (1 King).

Marriage is a big deal; you must remain faithful to one another. If not, then adultery will occur. And God does not like that at all. Marriage is the choice to spend the rest of your life with one person, which should not be taken lightly. The choice to have sex before marriage can impact the relationship you have with your spouse. As a teen, you probably don't have marriage on your mind, but you might think about love. You must know the difference between love and lust.

Avoiding Sexual Immorality

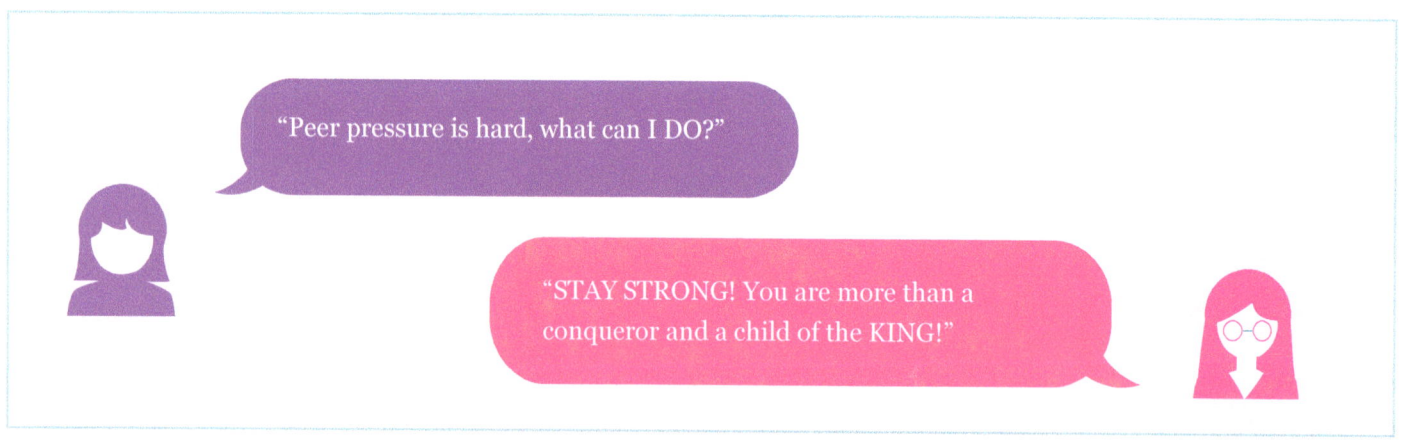

 Should I send a picture of my body to my boyfriend or friends? They say it cool to do.

 Run!! NO WAY NEVER
This is totally inappropriate, don't never display your body to no one."

Here are a few ways to help you fight temptation:

1. Find out what God's will for your life is. 1 Thessalonians 4:3-5 says, "It is God's will that you should be sanctified: that you should avoid sexual immorality; that each of you should learn to control his/her own body in a way that is holy and honorable, not in passionate lust."

2. The battle starts in mind. Be careful what you fill your mind with. When you drift off and think impure thoughts, get busy thinking of your future instead, like what college or trade school you want to attend. Take a walk, clean your room, and write out what you hope to achieve in the future in your journal. Or, read some good books.

3. Pray. Depend on God to give you the strength you will need in this battle (Matthew 6:13, James 5:16).

4. Don't get into tempting situations. It is helpful to read the bible daily. That way, you will have so much of the word on the inside, that when temptation comes, you will be ready. If temptation comes into your life, look for a way to escape. Set boundaries.

5. Never think that you are alone. You are not the only one that has ever been tempted. Talk to your mother, she will understand. Learn to know yourself. Know when you are vulnerable to temptation.

You will be tempted every day, but you can be prepared for it. Temptation is not only sexual desires. Drugs, and peer pressure are also forms of temptation. Don't you ever think that you cannot be forgiven. There will be times when you will fail; we all have. Remember to repent and ask God to give you the strength you need to discontinue the undesirable ways. Following God and fighting temptation can help you grow smarter and stronger. Seek professional help if needed. Do not be afraid to ask and tell a trusted adult what you are going through. Holding in your feelings will only lead to more problems.

Sexting

This is a trap of the devil to ruin your character. Sexting is not cool at all; it is when you are taking sexual images of yourself and sharing the images via text messages or posting them on the internet/social media. Sending a nude or a sexy selfie is risky, dangerous, and illegal as a young adult; others may pressure you into sexting, and they might make it seem like fun. Please don't believe it's an art of building self-confidence because it is not true. You have to think about what will happen if things end with your boyfriend or the word gets out. Others might share the sexual image to get revenge.

It's not okay to say "Okay" to sexting as you grow into an adult. This terrible decision can follow you for a lifetime. People you don't know can find such images of you. Data breaching and child molesters are lurking daily on social media, Snapchat, video games, chat rooms, and so many other platforms. Also, BE CAREFUL not to send or tell strangers your locations.

Risk of SEXTING:
- Losing respect from others.
- You become a victim of cyberbullying.
- Reputation is ruin.
- Can lead to mental health issues (depression, suicidal thoughts).
- Taking sexual pictures of anyone younger than 18 years old (including yourself) is considered child pornography. This is against the law.

Things to think about when sexting is being exposed to you.

- Be kind and show respect. In the electronic world, act the same as you would when you're face to face or if your parents were in the same room as you.
- Never think your messages or pictures will stay private. They may be copied, shared, or stored for later use.
- Say no when you're not comfortable with what is happening. Talk to an adult you trust about it.
- Be bold. Come up with a response for when you are asked to send a sext. E.G. "Sorry, I don't engage in sexting."
- Think before you send. How will others react? Your friends, family, or future boss might see it.
- Don't forward. Sharing sexts may be against the law.

Be smart and avoid unhealthy relationships that lead to the pressure of sexting.

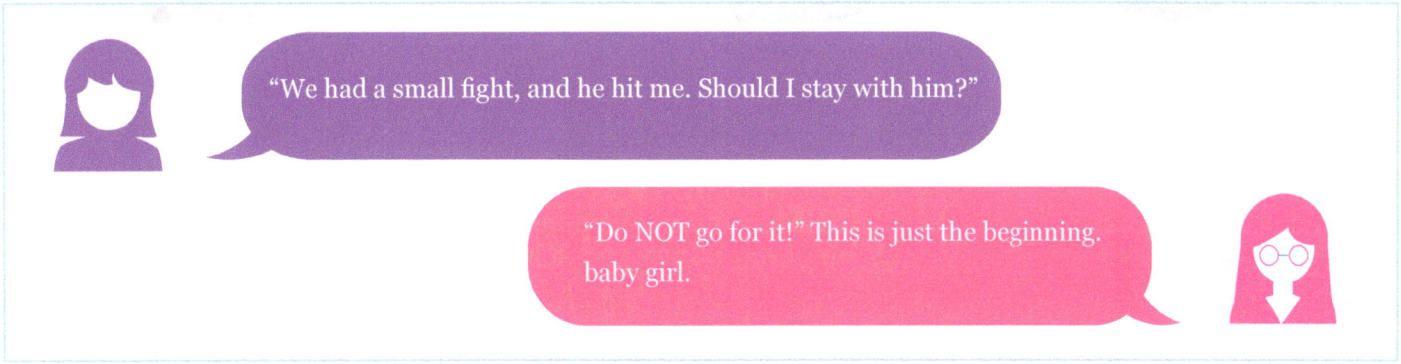

Domestic Abuse

Abuse can come in many forms: physical, emotional, and sexual are just a few. Do not allow anyone to abuse you. If it doesn't feel right, then it is wrong. In relationships, some guys feel the need to control you. No one can control you but you. Guys use sex as leverage to get you to do what they want. This is another reason why you should wait to have sex and get to know yourself better. It is difficult for many girls to disassociate sex with emotions when their hearts feel a connection. Since we are nurtured by nature, it's hard not to want to please someone we feel close to.

Relationship Abuse

Males view sex as an act of manhood. Get it, stick it and move on to the next one. Suppose you are in a situation where this sweet, nice boy starts to pressure you for sex. Put your foot down and tell him, "NO, and if you ask me again, you can find someone else." If he leaves, he wasn't the one. If he stays, make sure he knows you are very serious and that he shouldn't ask you again. If he starts to show signs of violence, then know that you cannot help this person; walk away. It can start as a push or pull, then he'll say, "Baby, I'm sorry. I will never do that again." The next time will be a slap, or he will hit you where no one can see, but you will be bruised. He will say, "I'm sorry. I'm just stressed out. I mean it this time, I will never do it again." All lies, and don't you dare put up with this kind of behavior. Then, he will get you far away from the people that love you and start telling you things to turn you against your close friends and family. He wants you to abandon them. He will say they are jealous, and they don't want to see you happy. He might even say, "Let's go away together and be happy!" REALLY! Do not fall for that. That is his way of getting you away from the protection of your family and the ones who care about your well-being.

Family Member Abuse

When most people think about a young girl getting abused, they immediately think of her boyfriend or partner. However, abuse is not limited to just romantic relationships.

If a male family member tries to sexually abuse you, seek medical and professional help. If it has already happened, tell someone and then seek medical and professional help. The abuser will try to convince you it was your fault, or he might threaten you if you tell. He might say something like, "I will hurt someone you love." Or he might even taunt you by saying that no one will believe you. That's all lies. Tell your mother and father. If you feel you cannot talk to them, talk to your counselor or pastor. If you find yourself in a predicament (raped) and the person has left, go to the hospital or police. Do not shower because all the evidence is on you, and you want this person to be caught. You are probably not the first person he has done this to, and if he is not caught, you won't be the last.

Get Help

Do not let anyone steal the bright light that shines in you. You have dreams and goals for your life and being with an abusive person can dim that light. These guys are sick and need professional help; they are battling something dark inside of them. Only a person who is trained to handle psychological dysfunctions can show them a way to conquer the evil inside. Maybe they were abused or seen someone close to them being abused as a child. They need help, but not from you. Pray for them and keep it moving. Your life is too precious and full of possibilities to take on the burden of another. Here is the National Violence Hotline number: 1-800-799-7233. Please call if you or someone you know needs to talk to a professional that can help.

Questions

Stage four of becoming a Butterfly is a lot to take in; that is why it is necessary to keep this book close by while you are going through your transformation stages.

1.   What are your likes and interests?

_____

_____

2. The person you are interested in, what are his likes and dislikes?

_____
_____

3. What is your belief or faith?

_____
_____

4. Do you do things because you want or because your peers do them?

_____
_____

5. When you are with that special person, do you feel at ease and comfortable? Or stressed and not your self?

_____
_____

6. What makes you happy?

_____
_____

7. What makes you laugh?

_____
_____

8. What is the one thing you dislike the most about others?

_____
_____

9. What does abuse look like and feel like to you?

_____

_____

10. How do you feel about intimacy, and how far will you go?

_____

_____

As you get older, your perception of dating will change. Feelings will change, and boys can be persuasive if you are not mature enough to say NO to things that make you feel uncomfortable. Sex is not a game, and you should want to save your temple for someone who is worthy and respectful towards you and your family. If you believe that Jesus Christ is the son of God, and God sent His son to die for our sins, and He will come again to judge the living and the dead, then you are a Christian. It is a little more than that but, if you believe in God, then you know He created you. And God doesn't make "NO JUNK." You are a queen, and you have a future waiting to be explored and conquered. You are not going to let anything, or any boy get in the way of your dreams. And if you are not a believer, this goes for you also.

You might think, "But that boy he's so cute and all the girls like him." So, what? Is he smart? Does he have a future? Is he respectful? Is he always talking about things that make you uncomfortable? Like, "I want to show you how much I love you by putting this thang on you?" NO! Does he want to touch you in places he shouldn't? When you say no, does he get an attitude? If so, walk away. I am going to be real and upfront. Boys will tell you anything they think you want to hear to convince you to have sex with them. Having sex can create babies. Babies are with you for life; they keep you up at night and will need attention all the time.

When you have a baby, you cannot hang with your friends, cannot go to parties, and most guys look at you as easy because they know you had sex. This does not mean you cannot like a boy; you just need to be smart about dating. Earlier, we talked about being a Christian; if you believe you were created by God and your body is your temple, then you have to have a different attitude toward dating. The bible doesn't tell you not to date; it gives you an idea of what God expects from you. If you are a non-believer or just don't have a clue, you should follow these guidelines on dating. Being a teen, you will form all kinds of relationships. These are the years you will start to build ties outside of the family. Always have a relationship with your mom so you can talk about how you feel about a special friend. Let's talk about the best way to know if the person you like is good for you.

Friends First

Did you know that friendship is the foundation to a good relationship? Think about what it means to be a friend. You tell each other everything; in fact, you can't wait to talk to each other. You appreciate the little things about each other. You encourage and uplift each other. Friendships are awesome. Being friends in a relationship is the most important factor for sex and longevity. Finding a partner who is first and foremost a friend can have countless benefits.

Friends often share common goals and interests. Friends can help you become more successful in school, and they can also help you network with others which can be very helpful later in life.

Relationships will be hard to build if you date people for only a short time since you won't know that person very well. It takes time to get to know who people truly are. Some guys can put on air to win you over. When you get your heart involved and find out that person is not who you thought he was, it will be harder to get out. Before you consider letting a person in your temple, get to know them for at least six months to one year. During that time, be observant and ask questions. You should learn to watch for signs that you do not approve of. If you have a gut feeling about something, do not ignore it. Be selective, don't just date the first person that asks you out on a date. Try to find someone you have chemistry with and is trustworthy. Date people your age or maybe a year or two older.

Some older males may be ready for a more intimate relationship and try to pressure you into doing things you are not ready for. Get to know a few people casually before you start anything serious. Dating is meant to be casual and fun at first, then it might develop into something more serious later. Don't force yourself into a relationship you are not feeling.

Remember, we all are different, and we have different likes, personalities, ideas and opinions. It's important to value each other with respect and honor. DO NOT EVER think you can change another person. People change on their own if they feel it is beneficial to their future.

Here are some major questions to ask while you are getting to know each other:

- Do you attend church?
- What are your spiritual beliefs?
- What are your values?

- How is your relationship with your mother?
- What's your view on college, trade school, or the military?
- What are your future goals?
- What is your view on spending money?
- Do you put money aside for the future?
- How is your relationship with your father?
- Do you drink or smoke?
- Do you have any pets?
- What are your political views?
- Do you play any sports?
- When you take time for yourself, what do you do? / What do you do during your alone time?

It take six months to a year to truly know the person you want to build a relationship with. During this time, you will also learn some new things about you.

If he doesn't have ambitions and future goals that match yours, maybe he's not the one.

Here are two movies about love, friendship and being true to you. They will teach you not to please others.

A must WATCH!

There are two movies that I want to recommend for you to watch: Beauty and the Beast and Easy A. Beauty and the Beast will show you how friendship can turn into romance. Easy A will show you that you can't help everyone, especially if helping them will hurt you. It will also show you how lying to help others can bring unwanted rumors and despair.

Drugs and Alcohol

> Everyone Is Doing Drugs, Should I?

Don't Believe the Hype
You might find yourself being very impressionable at this stage. You may notice that those around you, friends included, are trying drugs. Peers will offer you what may sound like an amazing experience. They are not going to tell you the truth. Their home life could be different from yours, and they could be looking for a way to escape the difficulties at home. Talk to your mom, aunt, grandmother, or a teacher you can trust and know is responsible if you are feeling pressured. Your mind and body are still growing and adding drugs and alcohol will slow the process.

Alcohol is created when grains, fruits, or vegetables have been fermented. The process that uses yeast or bacteria to change the sugars in the food into alcohol is called fermentation. It is used to produce many necessary items. Alcohol has different forms and can be used as a cleaner, an antiseptic, or a sedative.

You might be wondering, "If it is used as a natural product, why do I need to be concerned about drinking it?"

For starters, alcohol gets absorbed into the bloodstream. It affects the central nervous system (the brain and spinal cord), which controls all body functions.

> What Alcohol Does...

TRANSFORMATION THE YOUNG GIRL GUIDE TO WOMANHOOD 48

> Alcohol is a depressant, which means it slows the function of the central nervous system. Alcohol blocks messages trying to get to the brain. This alters your perceptions, emotions, movement, vision, and hearing.

Intoxication

Getting Drunk

Here are some ways alcohol can affect the body: slurred speech, stagger, loss of coordination, and disorientates. Depending on the person, intoxication can make someone talkative or very aggressive and angry. You might act totally out of character. This is also a time when you can be taken advantage of by your so-called friends, boyfriend, and even an unworthy family member because they know that your defenses are down. More often than not, depending on how much you drink, you might not even remember what happened the previous night which is why so many predators go after intoxicated girls.

If you want to try drinking, talk to your mother and be honest. Your first taste of alcohol should be around trusting, responsible, and caring adults at home. That way, if you get intoxicated, you will have someone who can help take care of you and not take advantage of you.

Drugs

There are many types of drugs, and teens will try anything to be cool or be accepted by their peers. Drugs affect each person differently. Some people might try it and find it is not for them and then quit, while others might go down a slippery slope and are unable to get back up to the top.

A beautiful, talented young lady had a promising future, but she wanted to be cool and fit in. She started taking drugs. It started with marijuana, then it went to pills and finally, crack. She is now in her thirties and is on the streets selling her body. She is living on the streets, having sex with whomever will give her ten dollars for a fix. She never thought her life would be this way. Don't let this be you. Don't go down that road.

The best way to stay cool is by being yourself. DON'T TRY DRUGS. It could cost you your future or your life. Different Drug on the Streets

Be Very Aware

Marijuana— can increase heart rate, respiratory problems, and mental illness. It can lead to poor judgment, decreased coordination, and trouble learning.

Vaping products— inhaling aerosol produced by an e-cigarette, hookah products, or similar device.

Cigarettes — they are more toxic now than they were in the 1950s. It can cause lung cancer, heart disease, and chronic obstructive pulmonary disease. They are very addictive

Other drugs that Teens Abuse

1. Adderall – Prescribed primarily for attention-deficit/hyperactivity disorder (ADHD). If they are taken any other way than prescribed by a physician, they can be dangerous and addictive.

2. OxyContin – Highly addictive drugs used to relieve pain. Teenagers tend to take with alcohol to increase the high. It causes confusion, slow pulse, lower blood pressure, poor coordination, slowed respiration, and lethargy.

3. Tranquilizers – Here are some examples: Xanax, Ativan, Valium, Phenobarbital, Ambien, and Sonata. These slow the central nervous system. Teens normally abuse them by taking too many in one sitting. They might also use them to bring down the high of other drugs. Some teens with anxiety find that taking tranquilizers help them decrease their anxiety so they will abuse them and end up getting addicted. They also increase drowsiness, poor coordination, along with slowed pulse and breathing.

4. Spice – Synthetic cannabinoids are not for human consumption. Here are some effects: high anxiety, paranoia, hallucinations, nausea, confusion, and violence.

5. Hallucinogens – LSD, mushrooms (Psilocybin), Peyote. Higher body temperature, poor coordination, poor judgment, anxiety, depression, and extreme paranoia.

6. Heroin – Very addictive drug. It can be smoked, snorted or shot in your veins with a needle. Here are some effects: nausea, vomiting, severe itching, increased drowsiness for several hours, slowing of the heart functions, and slow breathing. Mental function is also clouded. Some have reported getting skin infections. Death.

7. Date-Rape Drug – Gamma-hydroxybutyric acid also known as GHB—a hypnotic depressant. It comes in a liquid form that can be mixed with other liquids. Here are some effects: drowsiness, forgetfulness, loss of muscle tone, slowing of heartbeat and breathing. If it is severe enough, the victim could end up in a coma.

If you need help or you know someone who needs help, this is the American Addiction Center Phone Number: 877-959-7640.

Stage 3: Late Adolescents

Remember how we talked about the first two stages earlier in the book? Well as promised, here is the third. This third stage occurs from ages 18 to 21. Teens entering early adulthood have a stronger sense of their individuality now and can identify their values. They are able to make decisions on their own, without depending too much on the guidance of others. This doesn't mean that you shouldn't ask for help or advice when you need it, but you will become more independent and begin to get a good grip on who you are and what you want.

This will also be the time when your parents and/or guardians will expect more from you. They will ask you to help out around the house. Maybe they will ask you to do some chores on the weekend or maybe they will ask you to help your younger siblings with their homework. This may be a bit annoying to you at first because you want time to do your own things like hanging out with friends but see this as your parents giving you more trust. They see you as a responsible young adult now and that is why they will depend on you for help.

You are older now and you might realize you prefer for your space to be neat and clean when before, you didn't care. This might be especially true in the areas where you live, eat, and spend most of your time. Every teen should have responsibilities around the house. You should help with chores such as sweeping, moping, washing dishes, filling the dishwasher, or making sure the trash is taken out. If you drive, clean your car or offer to clean your parents' car for them. They will appreciate that. If you have pets, feed and take care of the pets without being asked. Picking up after yourself and others would also be helpful.

The next section will focus on being responsible and showing your parents that you are no longer a child that needs to be taken care of. This is important because the more responsible they see you being, the more they will trust you.

Why Being Responsible is Important...

Now that you have some ideas of what is happening with your body and mind, let's discuss being responsible and helping out around the house.

This will help you when you venture out to your new residence. Practice makes perfect, and there is no better place to practice like home.

Cleanliness is not just for self-appearance (looking good in front of others), but it is also crucial to your surroundings. Your bedroom, bathroom, and other areas of the house can use your assistance. Keeping your place clean is more than picking up clothes on the floor or bringing your food downstairs before bed (although keeping up these habits are great). You should be wiping down counters and disinfecting your place often to eliminate bacteria, dirt, oil, and dead skin cells (not to mention bugs and insects).

Have you ever gone to a friend's house and were scared to sit down because the house was filthy and smelly? Did you want to eat there or use the bathroom? Exactly. Do you understand why it is important now?
Please don't wait for an adult to tell you to clean; show them you are maturing and becoming more responsible by doing it without being asked first.

Before We Move on: Let's Do a Quick Check-in

Let's chat about you before we go on to the next section. What have you learned about yourself so far and what do you think about some of the things mentioned so far?
Exploring who you are, your likes and loves, and your beliefs can tell your story. In the section, it's time to take a deeper look at yourself.

Write down your feelings, tell your story, keep a diary and look at writing as an intimate way to reveal your secrets. Learn who you are and be comfortable with what you reveal about your desires, possibilities, and positive changes. Do not be ashamed or afraid of your new feelings and thoughts.

IT'S TIME TO TAKE A LOOK AT YOURSELF.

1. Are you distant or close with your family? Why?

_____

_____

2. Do you feel closer with your family or with your friends? Why? Write down your thoughts about both.

_____

_____

3. How important is your appearance and your grooming?

_____

_____

4. Is your appearance that important to you? Or is it only important because you care what your peers think of you?
_____
_____

5. What is it like to be YOU? Would being your true self affect your relationship with your peers?
_____
_____

6. Do you think you are unique? What makes you different from others?
_____
_____

7. Have you tried any of the substances mentioned above?
_____
_____

8. How did they make you feel? Would you ever try them again?
_____
_____

9. What does it mean to have a "natural high"?
_____
_____

10. Do you believe alcohol and drugs can affect your mind and body? Why or Why not?
_____
_____

Back to the Topic of Cleanliness

 How to Keep Your Room Clean

Make your Bed

 That bed is a mess!

The first thing you should do when you get out of bed is make your bed. Making your bed can make your room look neater. You should change and wash your sheets every two weeks (to get rid of the sweat, dead skin cells, food crumbs, etc that could collect on them). Unless you have an accident, then you should change them immediately; if you bleed on your sheets, soak them in cold water first, then wash them.

 Where is my pretty bra?

Keep your Clothes off the Floor:
Ask your mom for a hamper, then put all soiled clothes in it. Have a separate hamper for clean clothes-when you take your clothes out of the dryer and bring them into your room to fold. You do not want to use the same hamper for clean clothes and dirty ones.

Clean clothes should be put away right when it comes out of the laundry.

If you find yourself asking, "Where is my pretty bra?" almost every week, then that means you are not putting your items back where they belong. If you have a designated spot for your bras, then you will always be able to find your bras there. If the bra you are looking for is not there, then you will know that it is probably in your dirty hamper or in the wash.

If you don't have a dresser or much space to keep your clean clothes, here are some ideas for you:

- Use hooks on the wall for belts, scarves, bags, and more.
- Put bins in your closet floor for smaller items like socks, underwear, stockings, seasonal clothing, etc.
- Make sure you have plenty of hangers.

OH No! Is that a BUG?

No Food in Your Bedroom:
Avoid bringing any sort of foods and drinks (even a glass of milk) into your bedroom. A bowl of cereal, a piece of cake, or a sandwich can create crumbs that will end up on the floor. Despite how careful you are, just one crumb is enough to bring in a trail of ants. If you have to go to bed with a glass of water, remember to take that glass to the kitchen the next morning. Don't leave it sitting in your room.

Don't Forget to Donate
You are growing, and some items you wore maybe six months ago may be too small now. That's okay and is very normal. You should also consider doing some spring cleaning and look through your closet for items you no longer fit or no longer want to wear. Then, put all these clothes together and consider donating them to a shelter or to your local church (if they are taking donations).

After that, work on organizing all the clothes that you decided to keep. Here are some tips:

- Find a place for everything (that way you won't lose anything or find yourself being late for school because you can't find your favorite pair of blue jeans).
- Use labels (this is a quick and easy way to stay organized).
- Bins (bins are an inexpensive way to store smaller, seasonal clothing items such as beanies or bathing suits).
- Boxes drawers (boxes are a great way to bring some color and organization in your room. You can find box drawers in a variety of different colors).
- Shelves (a great way to display your items as well as organize them).

Get creative; bins are inexpensive and easy to put together. They come in primary colors and pastel colors.

Ouch! I stepped on a tack!

Vacuum your room weekly
When you walk into your room with your shoes on, whatever you tracked in from the outside will follow you inside. In order to keep your room clean, be sure to vacuum often. Vacuuming often will also ensure that you won't randomly step on a tack, pin, or nail on the floor.

Two things that vacuuming will accomplish:

- A freshly vacuumed room smells cleaner.
- When you vacuum, you will see a difference in the carpet, it will visually look cleaner.

If you don't have carpet in your room, then you can sweep and mop the floors once a week.

5-Minute Clean-Up:

Before you go to bed every night, do a 5-minute pickup. Put away items that are out of place. It won't take long, and you will wake up the next day to a clean room.

Unwanted and Unused Item:

It is easy to collect items without realizing it, from school papers to collectibles. Take time every few months to remove and trash unwanted and unused items. It would help if you did this every three month or so. The less items you have in your room, the neater your room will look. Having a clean room will make you feel better too. Being messy and disorderly is not hurting anyone but YOU. Eating in your room will bring in bugs, and bugs will bite you while you are sleeping; they will also crawl all over the room, leaving diseases. When you sleep on your bed sheets for longer than two weeks, you are sleeping on dead skin and dirt particles.

WHAT SHOULD YOU DO? Start by subconsciously getting up every morning and making your bed. Before you leave for the day, turn around and make sure everything is in place. If you had one of those days that was overwhelming and a little stressful, wouldn't you feel better coming home to a neat and clean room? Before you go to bed, take cups, glasses, and dishes to the kitchen. Then, pick up any trash and put them in the trash can. Put away any clothes that are just laying around and get your outfit ready for the next day. Finally, light a candle or use an infuser with your favorite scent and relax. You will sleep so much better this way.

Before we move on to talking about cleaning the bathroom, take a second to answer some of the questions below:

1. What do you need to do to get into the daily routine of keeping YOUR ROOM tidy and clean?
2. Is your room your safe haven?
3. How do you feel when you are in your room?
4. Write down a list of items you feel will make your room more comfortable and neater.
5. How good are you at getting rid of items you do not use or haven't used in over six months?

Germs in your Bathroom

Whether you have your own bathroom or whether you share one with everyone in the house, the bathroom harbors germs, like everywhere else in the house. Your body naturally carries germs; most germs are harmless, but not all of them are. .

It is kind of gross when you think about how many times you are in the bathroom and how many times you touch your face after.

Cleaning the bathroom weekly or two to three times a week can help when it comes to getting rid of germs and bacteria. The more people who use or share a bathroom (family, and friends), the more germs and bacteria will spread. Remember to wash your hands every time you use the bathroom.

Cleaning the bathroom is a MUST.

The Porcelain Throne:

Toilets can be dirty and can have some serious viruses if left unclean. You want to keep the toilet clean because this is where you sit. Some of the viruses include:

- Enteric bacteria: can cause gastroenteritis which causes your stomach and intestines to become irritated and inflamed, which will cause abdominal pain, diarrhea, and vomiting.
- Gastrointestinal illness: a virus caused by feces which is caused by poor hygiene habits. It can leave traces on toilet seats, countertops, and faucets.
- Salmonella and E-coli: other common bacteria found in and around the toilet area.

How to properly clean the toilet:

- Put on gloves.
- Wipe the toilet with a damp sponge.
- Apply toilet cleaner to the inside of the bowl.
- Scrub the bowl with a toilet brush.
- Flush the toilet.
- Clean the rest of the toilet with a disinfectant cleaner.
- Clean the handle thoroughly.

What about the shower?

The shower is the perfect environment for mold, mildew, and bacteria to thrive. The bacteria in the shower will not harm you unless you are unhealthy, or your immune system is weak.

Some people think they do not have to clean their shower because the water continuously runs out through the drain while showering, but that is not true. In order to combat bacteria, you should clean the shower at least twice a week. If you like taking baths, you should clean the tub after each bath to get rid of the dead skin cells and dirt that comes off your body during your bath.

How to clean the shower:

- Wipe down the bathtub, shower doors, and floors with a product approved to kill mold.
- Use a tub and tile cleaner.
- Grab a sponge meant for cleaning the shower (do not grab the sponge you use to clean the toilet).
- Remove everything from the shower-like shampoo, cleansers, and soaps.
- Thoroughly spray the shower walls and floor.
- If you have a removable shower head, use it to rinse the walls and tub.
- Don't forget to clean the showerhead.

Clean the sink the same way as the shower: wipe the countertops and the knobs. DO NOT USE the same sponge for the shower, tub, and sink that you used on the toilet.

Bathroom Towels:

Always hang your bath towel to dry after you are finished with it; if you leave it on the floor or bunched up in a corner, bacteria can fester quickly if the towel is not properly dried. After three uses, it should be washed. Never use the same washcloth to wash your face and your private area. When your cycle is on, you should have a washcloth for that area only.

Bathroom Floor:

Bath Mats and bath rugs will get wet, and walking on them can increase the risk of foot fungus. Wash these often and keep them as dry as possible.

For small bathroom floors, you can use a sponge. Use bleach and a disinfecting cleaner. If your bathroom is quite big, use a towel and wipe your way out of the bathroom (start from the point furthest from the door, then make your way out). Or if you prefer, you can use a mop or a Swifter.

Conclusion

I hope this book has helped you understand some of the transitions your body is or will be going through as you start to become a young woman. Watching your body change right in front of your eyes can be a beautiful, wonderful, and confusing time in your life. This is the time for you to embrace who you are and explore yourself for who you are becoming. It's also a great time to learn from the women around you. Changes in your body and mind are something you cannot ignore; they will happen. Everyone's experiences are different. Don't be afraid to talk to your mother, grandmother, or older sister.

Also, if you see friends or close family members doing things that are dangerous, speak up. Remember, "See something, say something." If you can't talk to anyone in your family, then befriend an older mature adult woman who will guide you during this time. Remember, your mother or female guardian should be your number one resource. She has gone through the same experience you are going through, and you are likely to share some similarities with her. If your mother is not in your life, then reach out to a trusted female adult. Sitting down and talking to her about feminine issues is a way of showing her you are maturing. Puberty, adolescence, and age doesn't make you an adult. Making mature, responsible decisions is the biggest part of adulthood.
When you get moody, and the world seems so far away, remember this is only for a short time. Don't let it defeat you or your joy. Take this time to write in your journal, clean your room, or do something nice for someone else. Like giving the clothes you can't fit in anymore to charity, helping your younger siblings with homework, taking a walk or talking to your grandmother about your family history. Ask her if she remembers going through what you are going through and how did she handle it? Don't let these two to four days out of the month determine who you are; you can beat them.

You can lay around in a dark, nasty room for those couple of days and get more depressed or you can open those blinds, clean up that room and feel better about yourself. When your room is dark and messy, that will make you feel worse. If your room is bright and clean, it can only help brighten your mood.

Don't ever use this time in your life as an excuse to be defiant, rude, or disrespectful. There is no need to have a nasty attitude. Sometimes, you will feel like being alone. You might feel sad, and you might not want to talk to anyone. When this happens, close your eyes, take in deep breaths, and let them out slowly. Always be honest and truthful but do it respectfully. Think about what you will say before you say it because words can hurt, and some things you can't take back. Teach yourself to control your emotions and feelings, especially during your cycle.

Make sure when your cycle is on, to keep the toilet clean. Blood seems to get in the most unusual places. Keep extra plastic bags in the bathroom so you can take your disposals (used pads and tampons) out in them.

Don't ever put that in the trashcan where someone can see it. Wash your hands often and drink plenty of water and cranapple juice, especially when your cycle is on. If your cramps hurt badly, you can try using a heating pad. To ensure that you will not stain your bed, wear an overnight pad, and put a towel under you. During the other times when you go to bed, if you wear PJ's, it is not necessary to wear underwear. If you wear a gown, this is the time for your body to air itself and breath while you sleep. This is not something you have to do, it is only a suggestion. When it comes to pads, tampons, sprays, and wipes, you decide what is best for you and what you feel most comfortable using.

I want you to feel just as comfortable about dating too. Always look for someone who is respectful and cares about your feelings and future. Do not settle for someone you know is not going to do anything with his life and will solely depend on you. You will be able to tell what kind of guy he is if you take the time to get to know this person. Demand respect, and don't allow anyone to treat you in any way that makes you feel uncomfortable.
I hope this book was a comfort to you. I hope it is one you can pass down to a younger sister or cousin. Maybe you will keep it and refer back to it when you feel any doubt. Learn what your morals and values are, and don't let anyone change you. Read and research and ask questions if you are not sure about something.
I love you and want the best for you because life is what we make it. Just do me one favor: Get up every morning and say, "Thank you, Lord, for your favor in my life. Guide me to be the best I can be, so I can inspire others with my actions and demeanor." Remember, you are now a beautiful butterfly, not a caterpillar. Spread your wings and FLY.

If this book has been helpful to you while you were/are going through your transformation, please leave a review at: gemlightpublishing.com.

Abstinence Contract

Abstinence Contract

I, _____, agree to abstain from (not use) any form of drugs, alcohol, or sexual activity while this contract is in effect.

I am a Queen, and I will conduct myself as one. I vow this contract to myself and God. This contract will be effective as long as I am under my parents' (or guardian's) care.

I AGREE:

1. To follow all rules and expectations at home and do chores assigned within my home.
2. To go to school daily, do all expected homework, and follow school rules and expectations.
3. To respect and follow all laws.
4. To be rigorously honest with my family at all times. I will tell the truth at all times and understand that omission (leaving something out) is a form of lying.
5. To communicate with my family members daily about what is going on in my life.

Signature: _____ Date: _____

Witness: _____ Date: _____

About The Author

Yolanda "BIRD" Bradley is a retired 7th-grade English teacher and a member of Delta Sigma Theta Sorority Inc. She attended Tennessee State University, where she obtained her Bachelor's in Speech & Communication. Ms. Bradley also received her Master's in Business Administrative Management at American Inter-Continental University.

Her education has provided many opportunities for her to give back to the youth and focus on adolescent girl's empowerment. She currently resided in Moss Point, Mississippi, with her son, who's hard at work on her next upcoming books.

References

Adolescence. Merriam-Webster.com. Retrieved 2019, September 22.

Arnett, J.J. (2007). Emerging Adulthood, What Is it and What is it food For? Child Development Perspectives. 68-73.

All About Periods. (2018, October) retrieved from Kidshealth.org

Buckner, Julia d. (2007, April 6) Marijuana use Mothers and Social Anxiety among Marijuana Using Young Adults.

Bradley, Nancy. (2018, October 26). Six rules for When Teens Start Dating. Retrieved from Better Homes and Gardens.

Dowshen, Steven. (2015, June). Common Puberty Concerns. Retrieved from KidsHealth.com

FamilyPlanning.org. "Changes at Puberty" Retrieved 2019, September 26

Great Dating Ideas for Teenagers. (1997). Retrieved from www.bygpud.com

J.J Bennett(2018, November 18, Retrieved from www.Kinbox.com, "Three Stages of Adolescence."

Lord Ph.D., Sarah, and Marsch Ph.D., Lisa. Emerging Trends and innovations in the Identification and Management of Drug use among Adolescents and Young Adults. (2011, December) Retrieved from pudmed.ncbi.nlm.nih.gov.

Steven, Dowshen, MD. (2015, June). Stages of Puberty Retrieved from KidsHealth.com

Sexual and Reproductive Health, Alberta Health Services (October 21, 2019.)

https://myhealth.alberta.ca/Alberta/Pages/Sexting-teens-and-technology.aspx

Teens: Alcohol and other drugs. (2018, December 27) American Academy of Child & Adolescent Psychiatry.

www.aacp.org/aacap/families_and_youth/facts guide/Teens-alcohol-And-Other-Drugs-003.aspx.

Timing and Stages of Puberty. (2014, May 23) Retrieved from GirlsHealth.gov.

The Emotional Signs of Puberty. (2017, July 04). Retrieved from Kidspot.com.au.

Why being a Friend First is Important? (2014, March 5). Retrieved from Good Therapy: Marriage and Dating.

When puberty starts for Girls. (2019, June 25). Retrieved from WebMD.com

Your Teen Relationship with Others. (2014, April 15). Stanford Children's Health/Puberty.

Sexual and Reproductive Health, Alberta Health Services (October 21, 2019.)

https://myhealth.alberta.ca/Alberta/Pages/Sexting-teens-and-technology.aspx

Credits:

I would like to thank the person who gave me the idea to write this book,
Erica Sherrill. She has been an inspiration to me in so many ways.

Design Credits: Ramsha Khalid

Cover Designer : Erica T Sherrill

My Personal Journal

Date: _____/_____/_____

My Personal Journal

Date: _____/_____/_____

My Personal Journal

Date: _____/_____/_____

My Personal Journal

Date: _____/_____/_____

My Personal Journal

Date: _____/_____/_____

My Personal Journal

Date: _____/_____/_____

My Personal Journal

Date: _____/_____/_____

My Personal Journal

Date: _____/_____/_____

My Personal Journal

Date: _____/_____/_____

My Personal Journal

Date: _____/_____/_____

My Personal Journal

Date: _____/_____/_____

_____
_____
_____
_____
_____
_____
_____
_____
_____
_____
_____
_____
_____
_____
_____
_____
_____
_____
_____
_____

My Personal Journal

Date: _____ / _____ / _____

My Personal Journal

Date: _____/_____/_____

My Personal Journal

Date: _____/_____/_____

My Personal Journal

Date: _____/_____/_____

My Personal Journal

Date: _____/_____/_____

My Personal Journal

Date: _____ / _____ / _____

_____
_____
_____
_____
_____
_____
_____
_____
_____
_____
_____
_____
_____
_____
_____
_____
_____
_____
_____
_____

My Personal Journal

Date: _____/_____/_____

_____
_____
_____
_____
_____
_____
_____
_____
_____
_____
_____
_____
_____
_____
_____
_____
_____
_____
_____
_____
_____
_____

My Personal Journal

Date: _____/_____/_____

_____
_____
_____
_____
_____
_____
_____
_____
_____
_____
_____
_____
_____
_____
_____
_____
_____
_____
_____
_____
_____

My Personal Journal

Date: _____/_____/_____

My Personal Journal

Date: _____/_____/_____

My Personal Journal

Date: _____/_____/_____

My Personal Journal

Date: _____/_____/_____

My Personal Journal

Date: _____/_____/_____

www.ingramcontent.com/pod-product-compliance
Lightning Source LLC
Chambersburg PA
CBHW051258110526
44589CB00025B/2865